6. Pray for
order to understand what yo
would be an appropriate vers

7. *Class teac*
study will find some helpful so

MW00987770

... page 41.

how to
take the self-check tests

Each lesson is concluded with a test designed to help you evaluate what you have learned.

1. Review the lesson carefully in the light of the self-check test questions.

2. If there are any questions in the self-check test you cannot answer, perhaps you have written into your lesson the wrong answer from your Bible. Go over your work carefully to make sure you have filled in the blanks correctly.

3. When you think you are ready to take the self-check test, do so without looking up the answers.

4. Check your answers to the self-check test carefully with the answer key given on page 48.

5. If you have any questions wrong, your answer key will tell you where to find the correct answer in your lesson. Go back and locate the right answers. Learn by your mistakes!

apply
what you have learned
to your own life

In this connection, read carefully JAMES 1:22-25. It is only as you apply your lessons to your own life that you will really grow in grace and increase in the knowledge of God.

1

Testing

Introduction (1:1)

The Writer

Modern opinion tends more and more to identify the writer as James, the Lord's brother (GALATIANS 1:19) not the James of the apostolic band.

Perhaps the special appearance of the risen Lord to the brother (I CORINTHIANS 15:7) qualified him for this work. He was put in charge of the mother church at Jerusalem.

Clement of Alexandria tells us that "Peter, James and John (the apostles most honored) chose James, the Lord's brother to be Bishop of Jerusalem after the Lord's ascension."

It should be noted that, after the death of the apostle James, the brother of John (ACTS 12:2), Peter sent the news to James, the Lord's brother (verse 17) at Jerusalem. Later at the Jerusalem Council (ACTS 15) this James summed up the discussion (verses 6-29) and formulated the letter which is striking in phraeseology as compared to the Epistle of James.

When Written

There is much to favor the view that this was the first Christian Epistle. If written before Paul's letters, the notion of some that there is contradiction between Paul's views and those of James, falls at once. James says much which supplements Paul's teachings. The careful student cannot fail to see that the language of James presupposes all evangelical doctrines as taught by Paul.

James was opposed to a lifeless, intellectual Christian profession and puts special emphasis on works as the fruit of faith and the evidence of justification. All is based on the new birth (1:17, 18, 21) and faith in Christ (2:1, 22) and carries no suggestion of salvation on the basis of works.

Contrasts

Just as the one gospel of Christ has been given four settings in the four records of Matthew, Mark, Luke and John, so the more advanced Christian truths are given different emphasis by the four writers—Peter, James, Paul and John.

James, like Matthew, had the Jew especially in mind. The problem of the Jew was that he meant well but had no power to perform (compare ROMANS 10:2, 3). James shows that a personal faith in Christ will put into the heart a desire to do His will and will give power unto righteousness.

There would have been something sadly lacking in the New Testament had there been no Epistle of James, for his message was especially helpful to the devout Jew in correctly understanding the gospel. There were those who argued that the Christian gospel had no place for good works: it was all grace and therefore not practical in its outlook. James shows that Christianity is GRACE AT WORK and that those who profess to be born of God, while manifesting no fruit in practical service to others, know nothing of the real *possession* of salvation.

1. Which "James" was the writer of this Epistle?

1:1 _____

2. What brothers did James have through his father, Joseph?

MATTHEW 13:55 _____

3. Were there also sisters?

MARK 6:3 _____

4. Even though he is Christ's brother, what is James content to call himself?

1:1 _____

5. For whom did James especially prepare this letter?

1:1 _____

3

After the captivities, the remnants of the twelve tribes became amalgamated. Tribal distinctions of territory had long since been lost at James' time. While Hebrews was written to the professing Christian Jews in Palestine, James writes to them wherever scattered.

Endure testing (1:2-12)

6. How should we respond to temptation?

1:2 _____

"All joy" is better rendered, "every kind of joy." There are varied elements of joy to be found in victory over the different forms of testing. The word here translated "temptation," as commonly used in the New Testament, stands for trials that take the form of suffering, rather than enticements to sin. Compare LUKE 22:28; ACTS 20:19; I PETER 1:6. This temptation might cause us to doubt God's readiness to help or His ability to work everything out for our good; therefore, it is the trying and the proving of our faith in Him.

7. Why is it that the believer, instead of sinking into a dejected state of mind, can count his testings a source of joy?

ROMANS 8:28 _____

8. Then what should the Christian do in the midst of suffering?

I PETER 4:16 _____

9. Toward what are his trials bringing him?

1:3 _____

10. What is the final product of patience?

1:4 _____

4

The final product of patience, perfection and entirety describes Christian maturity, not a state of perfect holiness.

11. What strength enables us to overcome temptation?

PSALM 71:16 _____

12. What part does self-reliance play in enduring temptation?

PROVERBS 3:5 _____

13. What is it that God is always willing to give us?

1:5 _____

Literally, "and doesn't scold one for asking."

14. How is it possible for a Christian to get divine discernment in matters that trouble him?

PROVERBS 2:3-5 _____

15. What does God have on deposit for all His children, in readiness for the needs that may arise?

PROVERBS 2:7, 8 _____

16. Give an example of one who claimed what this promise offers.

I KINGS 3:9-12 _____

17. How did God receive this petition?

I KINGS 3:10 _____

18. Considering these passages, what does wisdom mean in the Scripture?

19. What help is wisdom when temptation comes?

_____

20. What is the one condition which we must meet before we receive wisdom?

1:6, 7 _____

21. What does James compare to the tossing sea?

1:6 _____

22. How was Abraham an example of unwavering faith?

ROMANS 4:18-20 _____

_____

23. Who will not receive anything from the Lord?

1:7 _____

Do not overlook the emphasis put on faith at the very outset of this epistle. Both here and in verse 3 faith means a confidence in God's willingness and ability to help.

24. Describe a double-minded man.

1:8 _____

A literal translation of "double-minded man" is "one who has two souls"—or one whose mind is like that of two men.

Verses 9-11 discuss poverty and wealth, which are two temptations that often lead the Christian astray. James says "the brother in humble circumstances" should "glory in his elevation [as a Christian, called to the true riches and to be an heir of God]." He adds that "the rich [person ought to glory] in being humbled [by being shown his human frailty]."—Amplified New Testament

25. How long will the rich man have his money?

1:10, 11 _____

_____

26. Why shouldn't we seek either poverty or wealth?

PROVERBS 30:8, 9 _____

27. How do both James and Jesus regard the man who endures?

1:12; MATTHEW 5:11, 12 _____

_____

28. What does the man who endures receive?

1:12 _____

29. What should be our attitude when we are tempted?

I PETER 1:6, 7 _____

check-up time No. 1

You have just studied some introductory material about James and also some truths about testing. Review your study by rereading the questions and your written answers. If you aren't sure of an answer, reread the Scripture portion given to see if you can find the answer. Then take the following test to see how well you understand important truths you have studied.

In the right-hand margin write "true" or "false" after each of the following statements.

1. Solomon's wisdom was given to him by God in answer to his request. _____

2. James compares the double-minded man to twin mountain peaks. _____

3. James teaches that testing is something to be very upset about. _____

4. This epistle was written by James the son of Zebedee. _____

5. James addressed his epistle to the Jews of Palestine. _____

6. When tried and tested it is important to lean hard on one's own understanding of life. _____

7. The man who endures will receive a crown of liberty. _____

8. The Bible teaches that the Christian should seek to be either wealthy or poor. _____

9. The believer can know that God is working out all the circumstances of life for his own good. _____

10. One of God's purposes in testing His children is to produce patience in them. _____

Turn to page 48 and check your answers.

Temptation

Lusts that war against the soul (1:13-16)

1. When is a person really tempted?

1:14 _____

Here temptation has a different meaning. It is not a trial in the form of suffering, but it is the prompting of our sinful flesh. Temptation is not sin, but when we give the decision of our wills to gratify the carnal suggestion, then temptation brings forth sin.

2. Can anyone charge God with being the cause of their saying "yes" to the promptings of the old nature?

1:13 _____

3. Where lies the real root of temptation?

MARK 7:20-23 _____

4. Does the Christian still possess the old nature?

ROMANS 7:14-18 _____

Although Satan, in special instances, works upon the weaknesses of the flesh, for the most part he can leave us to the corruption of the old nature. James would have us feel the responsibility that rests upon *ourselves*. We cannot shift it to Satan.

5. When our own wills say "yes" to wrong desire, what is as good as accomplished?

1:15 _____

6. When a life is handed over to sin, what is certain to be the issue?

1:15; ROMANS 7:5 _____

7. How should we treat our sinful desires?

1:16; COLOSSIANS 3:5 _____

8. What is the proper alternative to the works of the flesh?

GALATIANS 5:16 _____

Know that God is the source of all good (1:17, 18)

9. Contrast God and Satan.

1:17; JOHN 8:44 _____

_____

Here James clearly states that God does not tempt men to sin as some think (1:13), but He is the source of all good things.

10. When we are related to God, what is our confidence?

1:17 _____

The word rendered "variableness" is a scientific term used of the position of the planets. It is suggested here by the use of the word "lights"—the heavenly bodies as light-givers. They have their changes but the Father of lights never moves (PSALM 33:11). "Shadow of turning" means "shadow caused by turning," the word for "turning" in the Greek being the word from which comes our word "tropic." These are changes due to the position of the planet. The word for "shadow" also is a scientific term applied to the effect produced on the sun's disc by the moon in an eclipse. James seems to say: Science deals with changing phenomena but faith rests on an unchanging God.

11. What is the believer's relationship to God?

1:18; John 1:12 _____

_____

12. Who gave us the right of sonship?

1:18 _____

13. What instrument does God use to bring us to Himself?

1:18; Romans 10:17 _____

14. When we are thus begotten from above, what is naturally expected of us?

1:18 _____

James saw in those being born again a kind of pledge of a fuller harvest of souls to follow. See use of the word "firstfruits" in Leviticus 23:10; I Corinthians 15:20; 16:15; Revelation 14:4.

You have just studied some important truths about temptation. Review your study by rereading the questions and your written answers. If you aren't sure of an answer, reread the Scripture portion given to see if you can find the answer. Then take the following test to see how well you understand important truths you have studied.

In the right-hand margin write "true" or "false" after each of the following statements.

1. God, who never changes, is always willing to give perfect gifts to His children, even those who are being tempted.   _____

2. All men are children of God.   _____

3. Many temptations have their roots in man's own corrupt nature.   _____

4. Under certain circumstances it is fair to charge God with tempting us.   _____

5. The Christian's old nature is completely removed at the moment of his conversion to Christ.   _____

6. God has every right to expect that His children will live fruitful lives.   _____

7. God's Word plays an important part in bringing men and women to God.   _____

8. The alternative to the works of the flesh is the fruit of the Spirit.   _____

9. Surrendering to evil desires leads inevitably to sin.   _____

10. The wages of sin is death.   _____

Turn to page 48 and check your answers.

Profession and Reality

Be a doing Christian (1:19-27)

1. What characterizes a Christian's speech?

1:19; PROVERBS 10:19 _____

From the general thought of the high ideal of life implied in new birth from God, James passes to the special aspect of that ideal which to him was very important—the use of the power of speech. Real Christianity is a very practical thing and affects speech as well as deeds, thoughts and motives.

2. What indicates a wise man?

PROVERBS 17:27 _____

Many have gained a reputation for wisdom merely by keeping their mouths closed. Many have little to say and spend all their lives saying it.

3. Where especially is it wise to listen carefully?

ECCLESIASTES 5:1 _____

4. Who acts foolishly?

PROVERBS 14:17 _____

5. What kind of people often have quick tempers?

ECCLESIASTES 7:9 _____

6. Can hot-headedness be acceptable to God?

1:20 _____

7. What must we set aside?

1:21 _____

The English word "naughtiness" was used as late as the sixteenth century as the eqivalent of "wickedness." Gradually it lost its sharpness until now it is used of the misdeeds of children. Weymouth renders: "Rid yourself of the vile and evil influences which prevail around you."

8. How does Paul express the same thought?

EPHESIANS 4:22 _____

9. What is the instrument which enables us to live a better Christian life?

1:21 _____

10. When the Word is engrafted into the soul, what is the effect?

JOHN 17:17 _____

11. When a Christian does not translate his knowledge of the Word into conduct, what is he doing?

1:22 _____

How many deceive themselves by equating regular church attendance with the Christian life. And how many fool themselves by thinking that an occasional emotional experience is a substitute for consistent Christianity. The smallest good deed counts more than church-going and more than a grand declaration of

14

faith. Both are very much needed, but they must be backed by action.

12. According to Jesus, what must follow hearing?

LUKE 11:28 _____

13. To what does James compare the person who is a listener only?

1:23, 24 _____

The words, "his natural face," in the Greek actually means, "the face he was born with." That which a man sees in God's Word is a revelation of himself as he is by nature.

14. What does this looking glass reveal?

PSALM 19:12 _____

The words, "whoso looketh into" in the original mean "whoso stoops down to take a close look into." This suggests a blessed curiosity. Do we give the Word this kind of attention?

15. What can we expect if we are faithful doers?

1:25 _____

16. Whose religious profession is utterly vain?

1:26 _____

17. What is a good daily prayer for Christians?

PSALM 141:3 _____

18. What will help every Christian to see good days?

I PETER 3:10 _____

_____

One's spirituality leaks out rapidly through a loose tongue. Discretion of speech is far better than fluency of speech.

19. If your religion is not merely talk, how will it manifest itself?

1:27 _____

_____

20. What invariably can be said of a true Christian?

JOHN 13:35 _____

21. What example has Christ set for His followers?

ACTS 10:38 _____

_____

True Christianity is not an affair just between the soul and God. There must be a third party to it—our fellowman—for it is life for others in Christ's name, issuing from the implanted life.

22. Does James imply here that one receives his salvation by doing these things, or that these things are the issue of a genuine experience in Christ?

1:27 _____

Do not imagine contradiction between James and Paul. Paul believed as much as James that faith will bear fruit; James believed as much as Paul that works without faith are of no effect to save anyone.

16

check-up time No. 3

You have just studied some important truths about true Christianity. Review your study by rereading the questions and your written answers. If you aren't sure of an answer, reread the Scripture portion given to see if you can find the answer. Then take the following test to see how well you understand important truths you have studied.

In the right-hand margin write "true" or "false" after each of the following statements.

1. A quick temper is inconsistent with godly living. _____

2. Wise men are often men of few words. _____

3. Reading God's Word is more important than obeying it. _____

4. James teaches that salvation is a result of good works. _____

5. A person who claims to be religious but who has no control over his tongue is self-deceived. _____

6. Peter reminded Cornelius that the Lord Jesus "went about doing good." _____

7. Social work should be left entirely to government agencies. _____

8. The Christian must "put off" evil behavior. _____

9. The Word of God must become engrafted into the life if a person is to really live a holy life. _____

10. James likens the man who reads the Bible but fails to relate what he reads to his life, to a sailor tossed on a stormy sea. _____

Turn to page 48 and check your answers.

The Royal Law

Avoid partiality (2:1-13)

1. What are we warned against?

2:1 _____

2. What example was set for us by Jesus Christ?

MATTHEW 22:16 _____

_____

3. What is true of hypocritical religious leaders? Why?

JUDE 16 _____

_____

4. How are we likely to treat the rich man who comes to worship?

2:2, 3 _____

Verse two implies that both persons were Christians. There is no common economic level that God intends to exist among Christians. One of large means can be a consecrated Christian and one of poorer circumstances may be singularly favored of God. If we forget that all who are born of the Spirit are "heirs of God and joint heirs with Jesus Christ" we will be likely to make serious mistakes about God's children. The eye that is filled with Christ will not see the kind of coat a man wears (word rendered "vile" here means "worn or shabby") or what kind of car he drives.

18

5. Regardless of outward circumstances, what is true of every child of God?

GALATIANS 3:28 _____

6. What are we when we make distinction between rich and poor?

2:4 _____

(Literally, "evil-thinking judges")

7. What two things belong to the poor who love Christ?

2:5 _____   _____

_____

Another translation is found in the New English Bible. "Has not God chosen those who are poor in the eyes of the world to be rich in faith and to inherit the kingdom he has promised to those who love him?"

People of wealth can be at a disadvantage (MATTHEW 19:23, 24). The poor have less to hinder spiritual progress. Note that the words "them that love him" guard against the impression that poverty apart from a relationship with Christ is sufficient title to an inheritance.

8. How had the rich been treating the Christians?

2:6 _____

_____

9. Generally, did the rich have any respect for the name of Christ?

2:7 _____

10. What law should govern our relation to a neighbor whether he is rich or poor?

2:8; MATTHEW 22:37-39; LEVITICUS 19:18 _____

_____

Note that we are not to love God "as ourselves" and not to love our neighbor with all our mind and soul. God stands first and alone.

11. What is supposed to be the first and all-inclusive fruit of the Spirit in one who has been born of God?

GALATIANS 5:22 _____

12. When we practice love what will others know about us?

JOHN 13:35 _____

13. Is it consistent for the Christian to disregard the royal law?

2:9 _____

14. If we offend one point of the law, to what extent are we guilty?

2:10 _____

15. What is the summation of the whole law?

MATTHEW 27:37-40; GALATIANS 5:14 _____

_____

In Galatians "the whole law" means the entire law governing human relationships, not including the first four of the Ten Commandments and other laws which govern our relationship to God. So whether we kill or commit adultery (2:11), we transgress the same law, the law of love.

16. What is the law which will judge Christians?

2:12 _____

Lehman Strauss comments, "What then is the 'law of liberty'? . . . Could it be that the law of liberty is an inward constraint instead of an outward restraint? We have learned that the royal law, according to the Scriptures, is the law of love. Now if I am truly born again, indwelt by the Spirit of God, a partaker of the very nature of God, then it follows that I will be perfectly free to do that which is right, not by restraint, but by constraint. Paul wrote: "For the love of Christ constraineth us . . ." (II CORINTHIANS 5:14). The royal law of love, controlling our lives, causes us to want to reflect the life of our Lord."

17. Who will be judged mercilessly?

2:13 _____

Verse thirteen from the Berkeley Version reads, "For the judgment is merciless to those who have practiced no mercy, whereas mercy triumphs."

Concerning the judgment, Guy H. King remarks, "The Christian needs to bear in mind that, as ROMANS 14:10 tells us, 'we shall all stand before the judgment seat of Christ.' True it is, blessedly true, that the believer has not to face the judgment of the Great White Throne, of which REVELATION 20:11 speaks—his eternal relationship with God, and his everlasting bliss in heaven, are alike gloriously assured, in response to his 'faith in our Lord Jesus Christ' mentioned in our first verse; but, for all that, he has a judgment upon his works, his behavior, since he became a Christian—that judgment which is so vividly described in I CORINTHIANS 3:11-15, and whose severity is so plainly indicated by verse 13 of this passage that we are studying." That judgment will be severe because many of us will be denied the rewards which have been promised to the faithful; many of us will be saved "so as by fire."

18. Who will be judged mercifully?

2:13 _____

Lehman Strauss observes, "Let us remember that 'mercy rejoiceth against judgment.' If I show mercy to the needy instead of sitting judgment upon them, I shall triumph in the end at the judgment seat of Christ. The apostle John says that love has boldness in the day of judgment (I JOHN 4:17). Outward actions show very clearly what a man is at heart now, as well as what his reward will be hereafter. When a Christian shows compassion on others at all times he looks forward to the judgment with calm confidence. A heart full of mercy has no fear of the day of judgment but rejoices in the face of it."

check-up time No. 4

You have just studied some important truths about partiality in the things of God. Review your study by rereading the questions and your written answers. If you aren't sure of an answer, reread the Scripture portion given to see if you can find the answer. Then take the following test to see how well you understand important truths you have studied.

In the right-hand margin write "true" or "false" after each of the following statements.

1. The Lord Jesus treated the rich and the poor alike. _____

2. Rich people tend to be more reverend than poor people. _____

3. The man who shows no mercy can expect no mercy. _____

4. A person may be looked upon as poor by men, but as rich by God. _____

5. One of the marks of an apostate is his deference to those he thinks will be of use to him. _____

6. Partiality is permissible under certain circumstances. _____

7. The Christian who pays special attention to the rich members of the congregation is wise. _____

8. The law of God may be summed up in the one word "love." _____

9. A person who breaks only one of God's commandments but who keeps all the rest has every cause to be pleased with himself. _____

10. Rich people are usually very generous in their attitude toward the poor. _____

Turn to page 48 and check your answers.

Faith and Works

Prove your faith by good works (2:14-26)

1. Are all people who *say* they are Christians necessarily born again?

2:14; MATTHEW 7:22, 23; TITUS 1:16 _____

2. Will a man of true faith distribute good advice and neglect material needs?

2:15, 16 _____

3. What is sure to happen to that kind of a person?

PROVERBS 21:13 _____

4. What is sure evidence of a counterfeit faith?

2:17 _____

5. How do Paul and John exhort all Christians?

TITUS 3:8; I JOHN 3:18 _____

_____

6. Does this mean that good works contribute to one's *salvation?*

TITUS 3:5; EPHESIANS 2:8-10 _____

7. What divine inducement encourages Christians to perform good works?

I CORINTHIANS 3:11-14 _____

8. What will happen if a child of God neglects many of his opportunities of service or fails to render the enduring service he should?

I Corinthians 3:15 _____

But James isn't concerned with the neglectful Christian; he is concerned with non-Christians who make a profession of faith.

9. What is visible evidence of genuine faith?

2:18 _____

It is unfortunate that people of the world sometimes have occasion to classify the good deeds of non-Christians to be worth more than the pious claims of some Christians who neglect doing good works.

10. Apart from saving trust in the Person of Christ, is intellectual assent to a dogma of any value?

2:19 _____

11. What is the term which describes someone who imagines that intellectual assent is enough?

2:20 _____

The word translated "vain" is one of contempt, meaning "empty-headed."

12. When James mentions Abraham's act of devotion in offering up his son as an evidence of faith, was he referring to the beginning of Abraham's relationship with God or to an experience many years later?

2:21; Genesis 22 _____

13. When Paul speaks of Abraham as an illustration of justification by faith, to what period in Abraham's life was he referring?

Romans 4:2-5; Genesis 12 _____

Note that Paul deals with the inward principle of salvation; James with the outward development and evidence of faith in Abraham's life many years after his original experience. When James speaks here of faith, he refers to the works of faith that result from acceptance of Christ. Paul in Romans four refers to the false notions that one by his good works can in some way contribute to the gift of eternal life. There is no disagreement between Paul and James. Abraham's faith was made evident by his works (2:22). Those who are on the Foundation, Christ (I Corinthians 3:11), will surely build upon it.

14. Would anyone ever have heard of Rahab's faith except that she expressed it in a good work, which was receiving and helping the Israelite spies?

2:25; Hebrews 11:31 _____

15. What does James compare with workless faith?

2:26 _____

James condemns the deadness of mere orthodoxy and formality where there is no saving faith in Christ.

check-up time No. 5

You have just studied some important truths about faith and works. Review your study by rereading the questions and your written answers. If you aren't sure of an answer, reread the Scripture portion given to see if you can find the answer. Then take the following test to see how well you understand important truths you have studied.

In the right-hand margin write "true" or "false" after each of the following statements.

1. Abraham's "good works" mentioned in Genesis 22 were the basis on which God saved him. _____

2. James is concerned with people who profess to be Christians but are actually unsaved. _____

3. A person's faith is proved by his works. _____

4. A person who says that he believes but who never behaves like a Christian is deceived. _____

5. Rahab's high moral character was the reason for her salvation. _____

6. Faith without works is dead. _____

7. Paul's references to Abraham's faith referred to a much earlier time in Abraham's life than the time referred to by James when he speaks of Abraham's works. _____

8. An intellectual grasp of truth is quite acceptable to God as a basis for salvation. _____

9. Good works contribute to salvation. _____

10. Christians who pass up opportunities to do good will be faced with their neglect at the judgment seat of Christ. _____

Turn to page 48 and check your answers.

Hold Your Tongue

Discipline your tongue (3:1-12)

1. Why should one consider the matter very carefully before entering into the field of Christian teaching?

3:1 _____

The word rendered "master" means "teacher."

2. How can a teacher avoid being a hypocrite?

ROMANS 2:21 _____

_____

3. Before we can become spiritual leaders, what must we receive from God?

I CORINTHIANS 12:28; EPHESIANS 4:11, 12 _____

_____

Many religious teachers who think themselves the messengers of God are really the instruments of Satan. Because they mislead others spiritually, great is the harm they do and terrible their fate.

4. What knowledge should keep all of us from being quick to assert our goodness?

3:2; ECCESIASTES 7:20 _____

_____

5. What is one of the first ways that we betray our shortcomings?

3:2 _____

6. What would be true of someone who could control his tongue?

3:2 _____

7. Why must we be careful in our speech?

3:2 _____

8. What terrific importance can there be in words?

Matthew 12:37 _____

9. What illustration does James borrow from the Old Testament?

3:3; Psalm 32:9 _____

_____

10. How does James further illustrate the power of little things?

3:4 _____

11. What is the next figure of speech that demonstrates the power of the tongue?

3:5 _____

Literally, "A little fire kindles how great a mass of timber." The word rendered "matter" means primarily wood in growth.

12. What may be the consequences of words carelessly spoken?

3:6 _____

_____

13. What is the source of defiling speech?

3:6; Proverbs 26:20 _____

14. What is especially true of an ungodly person?

Proverbs 16:27 _____

15. What kind of person will God punish?

PSALM 101:5 _____

16. What is another comparison that illustrates the difficulty of controlling the tongue?

3:7, 8a _____

17. But can man tame his tongue?

3:8 _____

Besides wild animals, man has tamed steam, electricity and atomic energy, but has failed to make any progress in controlling the tongue.

18. Who alone has power to bring our tongues under control?

PSALM 19:13, 14 _____

19. What is the effect of the undisciplined tongue upon others?

PSALM 140:3 _____

20. To what extreme can the undisciplined tongue go?

3:9 _____

21. What makes it a serious offense to curse a human being?

3:9; GENESIS 1:26 _____

22. Considering we ought to reflect Christ's life, to what kind of inconsistency may cursing be compared?

3:11, 12 _____

---

23. How should Christians be known?

MATTHEW 7:16, 17 _____

Seek true wisdom (3:13-18)

24. How should a man make evident his wisdom?

3:13 _____

"Conversation" in the King James is better translated "behavior."

25. What automatically negates any claim to superior wisdom?

3:14 _____

26. How does James describe this counterfeit wisdom?

3:15 _____

27. What do jealousy and rivalry always bring with them?

3:16 _____

28. What are the characteristics of real wisdom?

3:17 _____

_____

29. What must we do to reap the fruits of righteousness?

3:18: ISAIAH 32:17 _____

James speaks of wisdom as do the writers of Job and Proverbs; all three agree that it is the gift of God which is to be sought by earnest prayer. In Old Testament usage it has a wide meaning involving an understanding of the arts and sciences, but most stress is laid upon spiritual wisdom. This spiritual wisdom is fear of the Lord, which is made evident in the life of modesty, simplicity and devotion to God.

The conclusion of the chapter is that peace provides the seed-bed in which righteousness can be sown. This is God's use of the tongue—to say those things which promote heart-peace and righteousness (MATTHEW 5:9).

31

check-up time No. 6

You have just studied some important truths about holding your tongue. Review your study by rereading the questions and your written answers. If you aren't sure of an answer, reread the Scripture portion given to see if you can find the answer. Then take the following test to see how well you understand important truths you have studied.

In the right-hand margin write "true" or "false" after each of the following statements.

1. Most people can tame their tongues if they try hard enough. _____

2. Wisdom that comes not from God is earthly, sensual and devilish. _____

3. It is a dangerous thing to fail to practice what you preach. _____

4. A good test of a person's conduct is his conversation. _____

5. A person who can bridle his tongue can rein in his whole body. _____

6. Cursing is justified if there is sufficient provocation. _____

7. We will be judged for our works but not for our words. _____

8. A piece of gossip passed along may soon spread completely out of control. _____

9. Thoughtless words can have a defiling effect on a person's whole body. _____

10. True wisdom comes only from God. _____

Turn to page 48 and check your answers.

The Danger of Worldliness

Worldliness and Godliness (4:1-10)

Here we have a sudden transition from the subject of peace-makers (3:18) to that of the real cause of fighting (4:1). James has reproved believers for envy and party strife in 3:16.

1. To what can all conflicts within the church be traced?

4:1 _____

We can look to the fleshly nature as the cause of all quarrels within the church. The word rendered "fightings" means "brawlings"—bitter disagreements. The word here for "wars" is taken by many to refer to the bitter contentions between Jewish believers at the time—hot arguments over the sabbaths, feast days, etc. There are no wars more trying than religious controversies.

2. What have men always done instead of asking God's help?

4:2 _____

3. Are their lusts fulfilled and their strifes successful?

4:2 _____

4. How does God regard those who allow the Adamic spirit of hate to rule in their hearts?

I JOHN 3:15 _____

5. But when lustful people do ask something of God, why is it that they receive nothing?

4:3 _____

In other words, it is asked merely for the satisfaction of the fleshly nature.

6. Have men a right to expect anything from God when they have considered nothing but their own selfish desires?

MICAH 3:4 _____

7. What is the source of our highest and most permanent good?

1:17 _____

8. If we want God's best, what must we be willing to do?

I JOHN 3:22 _____

_____

9. What can interrupt our fellowship with God?

4:4 _____

Literally "wills to be." It is no iron fate. One's own will determines whether or not he will follow with the world's crowd. He soon finds that by such a choice he has antagonized the Holy Spirit and can find no heart rest for himself.

10. How does James address those of us who have lost this fellowship?

4:4 _____

This might make it appear that James was not here addressing true Christians. Note, however, that the better manuscripts have "adulteresses" only and the use of the feminine in this connection suggests the rendering:

34

"Ye adulterous souls." The reference is to the soul's unfaithfulness to God, as that of a wife toward her husband. This is a charge that can all too often be made against members of the household of faith, when, like Peter, they have followed afar off, controlled by the carnal nature.

11. Can one know the presence of God's love as long as he sets his affections on the pleasures of this world?

I JOHN 2:15 _____

The triple root of sin is (1) the world about us (4:4), (2) the fleshly nature within (GALATIANS 5:17), 3) the devil outside (EPHESIANS 6:11, 12).

12. What are the Old Testament words?

4:5 _____

This passage is not a quotation from Old Testament Scripture but a summary of its teaching. The Cambridge Bible says: "The true meaning and connection is: 'The Spirit which he implanted in us yearns tenderly over us'—that is, that we should live out His life." Darby's rendering is: "He yearns jealously for the Spirit he set within us" and Alford gives: "The Spirit who dwelleth in us jealously desires us for his own." The thought would be that the Father yearns to have all His own under the Spirit's control.

13. What must the Christian be especially careful to avoid?

EPHESIANS 4:30 _____

14. Since God loves His own with a feeling analogous to jealousy, how does He meet every humble surrender to His Spirit?

4:6; PROVERBS 3:34; I PETER 5:5 _____

15. What is it that will withhold His blessing from us?

4:6; Psalm 138:6 _____

St. Augustine said of pride: "That which first overcame man is the last sin he overcomes." It keeps one from the riches of grace. There are many sins against God's *laws* but pride is a sin against His *sovereignty*.

16. How do we overcome that self-assertive spirit within us?

4:7 _____

17. How do we put the devil to flight?

4:7 _____

18. Upon what will the strength of our resistance depend?

4:7, 8 _____

19. What is our defense against the devil?

I Peter 5:8, 9 _____

James brings out the truth that we must ask God's help and receive his strength by submission to Him. In Peter we learn that being armed with God's strength, we are prepared to assume the responsibility of being watchful and wise. With God's strength and our care the devil is put to flight.

20. In James' call to repentance, what is meant by "cleanse your hands"?

4:8; compare Psalm 24:4 _____

21. How should the repentant sinner express his sorrow?

4:9 _____

22. What should characterize our life in attitude and action?

4:10; MATTHEW 23:12 _____

Judge not the brother (4:11, 12)

23. What are we commanded not to do?

4:11 _____

The word translated "speak not evil" in verse 11 is rendered "back-bite" in ROMANS 1:30 and II CORINTHIANS 12:20.

24. What law do we break when me malign a brother?

4:11; LEVITICUS 19:18; MATTHEW 7:1-5; JAMES 2:8 _____

Charles R. Erdman says, "Of course, the law to which James refers is the law of love, 'the royal law,' 'thou shalt love thy neighbor as thyself.' One who is unkind in his criticisms not only breaks this law, but he condemns it as too high in its requirements or as unwise or unnecessary; he says in effect that he is superior to the law of love; he seems to argue that while it may be a good law for some people at some times, a superior person like himself cannot be bound by it, particularly in this imperfect world where some people need to be disciplined by his severe rebukes and punished by his stinging tongue. James intimates that, to say the least, it is better to keep the law of love than to try to find exceptions to its universal obligation."

25. What do we presume to be when we malign the brother?

4:11, 12 _____

_____

Do not be confident of the future (4:13-17)

26. Why should we not be confident that our plans must come to pass?

4:13, 14 _____

_____

27. How is fog compared to life?

4:14 _____

28. What ought we to say when we make plans?

4:15 _____

29. What is it when we neglect opportunities for service?

4:17 _____

We cannot forget that omission of known duty is sin as much as lying or stealing. Our neglect results in countless numbers of lost souls, whose blood is on our hands.

check-up time No. 7

You have just studied some important aspects about the dangers of worldliness. Review your study by rereading the questions and your written answers. If you aren't sure of an answer, reread the Scripture portion given to see if you can find the answer. Then take the following test to see how well you understand important truths you have studied.

In the right-hand margin write "true" or "false" after each of the following statements.

1. Human life is as fleeting as a vapor. _____

2. To fail to seize opportunities for doing good is sin. _____

3. The Holy Spirit can be grieved by believers. _____

4. Church squabbles arise out of the carnal hearts of men. _____

5. Prayers are often unanswered because of wrong motives in asking. _____

6. Worldliness in a believer breaks his fellowship with God. _____

7. The way to overcome Satan is by ignoring his attempts to overcome us. _____

8. James describes worldliness as spiritual infidelity. _____

9. It is wise to make big plans for the future without taking God into account. _____

10. The Holy Spirit longs to exercise complete control over the heart and life of every child of God. _____

Turn to page 48 and check your answers.

Closing Exhortations

The judgment of the godless rich men (5:1-6)

James is addressing the godless rich, not the devout well-to-do.
God has prospered many who have used their wealth for the service of Christ. If wealth comes to us, it is our responsibility to use
it for His work.

1. What will eventually be the fate of all whose lives are centered
upon wealth?

5:1; PSALM 49:16, 17 _____

_____

2. What is certain about those who set their affections on material
things?

I TIMOTHY 6:9 _____

3. What is already so certain that it can be spoken of in the past
tense?

5:2 _____

4. What two evidences will be used against rich men at the
judgment?

5:3, 4 _____

_____

_____

5. What title is here given the Lord?

5:4 _____

This title is appropriate because it means the "Lord of armies," who as Commander of the angelic hosts is fully able to respond to cries of injustice. "Sabaoth" is used twice in Scripture, once by James and once by Malachi, last of the prophets, who saw God as Judge on the last day.

6. How has the sinner used his wealth?

5:5 _____

_____

7. But how should the wealthy Christian expend his money?

I TIMOTHY 6:17-19 _____

_____

8. How has the just man reacted to oppression?

5:6 _____

_____

Look for Christ's coming (5:7-11)

9. What hope of the Christian makes oppression bearable?

5:8 _____

10. Who illustrates the patience of a Christian?

5:7 _____

In Palestine there are two rainy seasons, the early rain—October to February, and the latter—March to April. The Palestinian farmer must wait patiently for them, because nothing he can do will bring them sooner.

11. What assurance do Christians have that Christ will return?

Acts 1:11 _____

_____

12. What group of men serves as an example of patience?

5:10 _____

13. What man is a special example of standing firm?

5:11 _____

Sing and pray (5:12-18)

14. What should never be present in our speech?

5:12; Matthew 5:33-37 _____

_____

15. When afflicted perhaps to exasperation, what should the Christian do?

5:13 _____

Those who are exasperated are prone to use rash oaths. There is no reference here to solemn judicial affirmations. Our Lord answered a question on oath before Caiphas (Matthew 26:63, 64). And Paul used oaths in making solemn declarations (II Corinthians 1:23; Romans 1:9; Galatians 1:20; Philippians 1:8).

16. And when the Christian is happy, how should he express his happiness?

5:13 _____

17. How else can we express praises besides in song?

PSALM 107:2 _____

18. If a brother is sick, who should offer special prayer for him?

5:14 _____

19. What symbolic act were these spiritual leaders to perform?

5:14 _____

20. Who were first instructed to anoint with oil when dealing with the sick?

MARK 6:13 _____

Within the limits of the New Testament the Jerusalem church had only apostles and elders. The latter were to be mature believers appointed to spiritual oversight of the local flock. A concordance study of the word "elder" will show their functions. It is definitely implied that afflicted believers turned to an organized body of Christians for intercession.

21. Does this verse fourteen prohibit consulting a physician or dentist?

_____

22. What specifically were the elders to do with the oil?

5:14 _____

In some cases, oil was used for medicinal purposes (LUKE 10:34;

43

Isaiah 1:6). But here it is used symbolically—not as an oil rub or internal medicine but as an anointment for the head.

23. Of what was this outward sign expressive?

5:15, first clause _____

24. Was the effect dependent on the anointing, or what actually is the instrument of recovery?

5:15 _____

It does not say "oil and faith."

25. How soon may there be recovery?

Acts 9:34 _____

26. When a group of believers meet for prayer, on what does a positive answer depend?

Matthew 18:19 _____

27. Is the agreement just an arbitrary decision of individuals to ask for a certain thing? If not, what guides the agreement?

Proverbs 16:1 _____

28. So when can we be certain that we are to receive the very thing asked?

I John 5:14, 15 _____

29. Who teaches us God's will?

Ephesians 6:18; Jude 20 _____

30. Need we confine ourselves to official elders for help?

5:16 _____

31. Whose prayer is effective?

5:16 _____

The words here rendered "fervent and effectual" are one word in
the original, a word which means neither fervent nor effectual but
"working" or 'inworking." The American Standard Version of
1901 gives: "The supplication of a righteous man availeth much in
its working." Several authorities, however, have seen in this text
the thought of an "inwrought" prayer or "energized" prayer. It is
the Spirit-taught prayer of a righteous man that availeth much.

32. In whom have we an example of prayer power?

5:17 _____

Help save the sinner (5:19, 20)

33. What does a Christian accomplish when he permits himself to
be used in the conversion of a sinner?

5:19, 20 _____

_____

Most authorities understand verse twenty to mean that the sins
which are covered are those of the person converted, not those of
the converter.

Strangely there is no formal closing of the epistle as in all other
New Testament writings.

check-up time No. 8

You have just studied some important truths about God's judgment on the rich in the last days and also some vital truths on prayer. Review your study by rereading the questions and your written answers. If you aren't sure of an answer, reread the Scripture portion given to see if you can find the answer. Then take the following test to see how well you understand important truths you have studied.

In the right-hand margin write "true" or "false" after each of the following statements.

1. It is legitimate for Christians to use an expression such as "by heaven." _____

2. Prayer and praise are ways in which Christians should give expression to excessive feelings of joy or sorrow. _____

3. James recommended the use of special ointments in treating the sick. _____

4. James uses the farmer and the prophet as an illustration of Christian joy. _____

5. James uses Moses as an example of a man who had great power with God in prayer. _____

6. Wealth can make men happy. _____

7. Oppressed people are encouraged to look for the Lord's coming. _____

8. God will certainly judge those who are absorbed in a materialistic way of life. _____

9. The Bible ignores employer-employee relationships. _____

10. To spend money extravagantly on pleasure is a sin. _____

Turn to page 48 and check your answers.

Suggestions for class use

1. The class teacher may wish to tear this page from each workbook as the answer key is on the reverse side.

2. The teacher should study the lesson first, filling in the blanks in the workbook. He should be prepared to give help to the class on some of the harder places in the lesson. He should also take the self-check tests himself, check his answers with the answer key and look up any question answered incorrectly.

3. Class sessions can be supplemented by the teacher's giving a talk or leading a discussion on the subject to be studied. The class could then fill in the workbook together as a group, in teams, or individually. If so desired by the teacher, however, this could be done at home. The self-check tests can be done as homework by the class.

4. The self-check tests can be corrected at the beginning of each class seccion. A brief discussion of the answers can serve as review for the previous lesson.

5. The teacher should motivate and encourage his students. Some public recognition might well be given to class members who successfully complete this course.

Moody Press, a ministry of the Moody Bible Institute, is designed for education, evangelization and edification. If we may assist you in knowing more about Christ and the Christian life, please write us without obligation to: Moody Press, c/o MLM, Chicago, Illinois 60610.

answer key

to self-check tests

Be sure to look up any questions you answered incorrectly.

Q gives the number of the test *question*.

A gives the correct *answer*.

R *refers* you back to the number of the question in the lesson itself, where the correct answer is to be found.

Mark with an "x" your wrong answers.

TEST 1			TEST 2			TEST 3			TEST 4		
Q	A	R	Q	A	R	Q	A	R	Q	A	R
1	T	16	1	T	10	1	T	6	1	T	3
2	F	21	2	F	11	2	T	2	2	F	9
3	F	6	3	T	1	3	F	11	3	T	17
4	F	2	4	F	2	4	F	22	4	T	7
5	F	5	5	F	4	5	T	16	5	T	3
6	F	12	6	T	14	6	T	21	6	F	1
7	F	28	7	T	13	7	F	22	7	F	6
8	F	26	8	T	8	8	T	7	8	T	15
9	T	7	9	T	5	9	T	9	9	F	14
10	T	9	10	T	6	10	F	13	10	F	8

TEST 5			TEST 6			TEST 7			TEST 8		
Q	A	R	Q	A	R	Q	A	R	Q	A	R
1	F	12	1	F	18	1	T	27	1	F	14
2	T	9	2	T	26	2	T	29	2	T	15
3	T	1	3	T	1	3	T	13	3	F	23
4	T	4	4	T	5	4	T	1	4	F	10
5	F	14	5	T	7	5	T	5	5	F	32
6	T	15	6	F	20	6	T	9	6	F	1
7	T	13	7	F	8	7	F	17	7	T	9
8	F	10	8	T	11	8	T	10	8	T	2
9	F	6	9	T	12	9	F	26	9	F	4
10	T	8	10	T	28	10	T	12	10	T	6

how well did you do?

0-1 wrong answers—excellent work

2-3 wrong answers—review errors carefully

4 or more wrong answers—restudy the lesson before going on to the next one